RECORDERS

by Kara L. Laughlin

Published by The Child's World®
1980 Lookout Drive • Mankato, MN 56003-1705
800-599-READ • www.childsworld.com

Design element: Vector memory/Shutterstock.com
Photo credits: Alenavlad/Shutterstock.com: 21 (oboe); Andrea Nissotti/Shutterstock.com: 21 (flute);
Boris Medvedev/Shutterstock.com: 21 (piccolo); Chromakey/Shutterstock.com: 21 (clarinet);
furtseff/Shutterstock.com: 21 (bassoon); horiyan/Shutterstock.com: 21 (saxophone); Inspirestock
International/123RF: 14, 18; KPG_Payless/Shutterstock.com: 4; Lars Hallstrom/Shutterstock.com:
11; Martin Gerner/123RF: 8; MIGUEL G. SAAVEDRA/Shutterstock.com: cover, 1; Sarah Marchant/
Shutterstock.com: 12; Sergey Fedoskin/123RF: 7; Wilawan Khasawong/123RF: 17

ISBN: 9781503831902
LCCN: 2018960556

Printed in the United States of America
PA02417

Table *of* Contents

CHAPTER ONE

The Recorder

A group of children stands on a stage. They are playing recorders. They hum. They sing. They tap their feet. But mostly, they blow.

Recorders are part of the flute family. All flutes have holes. Recorders make music when air rushes past their holes. Just like flutes, recorders are instruments called **woodwinds**.

❮ *Recorders come in lots of different colors.*

CHAPTER TWO

The Holes

A recorder has eight holes for playing. Seven holes are on the front. One hole is on the back. Players use their thumb to cover this hole.

Players put fingers over the holes to change the recorder's **pitch**. This makes different musical **notes**.

The last two holes on some recorders are double holes. Covering these holes can make half-note sounds.

This recorder is made of wood. ❯

CHAPTER THREE

Playing the Recorder

To play a recorder, a person blows into the **mouthpiece**. When all the holes are covered, the recorder plays a low note. When all the holes are open, it plays a high note.

Recorder players might flutter their tongues to make different effects.

❮ *You don't have to always follow music written by other people. You can make up your own tunes!*

CHAPTER FOUR

A Beak and a Bell

A recorder's mouthpiece is like a whistle. A plug of wood called the **block** aims air at a sharp edge. This makes the air **vibrate**. The vibrating air makes the recorder's sound.

The **bell** is the bottom part of the recorder. This is where the air comes out. Sometimes players cover the bell. This can make a very high note or very low one.

In France, the recorder is called the flûte à bec or "beaked flute." That's because the mouthpiece looks a little like a bird's beak.

Recorder mouthpieces come in many shapes and sizes. ❯

CHAPTER FIVE

A Very Old Instrument

People have played recorders for hundreds of years. The first recorders were played in the **Middle Ages**. Recorders have not changed much. At first, most recorders were made of wood. Today, recorders are made of wood or plastic.

England's King Henry VIII (1491–1547) liked to play the recorder. By the time he died, he owned 76 recorders.

❰ *This actor is playing the recorder at a fair celebrating the Middle Ages.*

CHAPTER SIX

Recorders in Schools

Many kids learn to play the recorder in school. Plastic recorders are not costly. They have a pretty good sound. Most people can play a tune right away. These things make recorders a good first instrument.

People started making plastic recorders in the 1960s.

❮ *Children often learn to play the recorder before they are ten years old.*

CHAPTER SEVEN

One Shape, Many Sizes

Recorders come in many sizes. The smallest is about 6 inches (15 cm) long. The biggest is taller than an adult. Small recorders play high notes. Big ones play deep notes. Most of the time, several recorders of various sizes are played together in bands.

The subcontrabass recorder is the largest recorder. It is almost 10 feet (3 m) tall!

Larger recorders need special mouthpieces. ❯

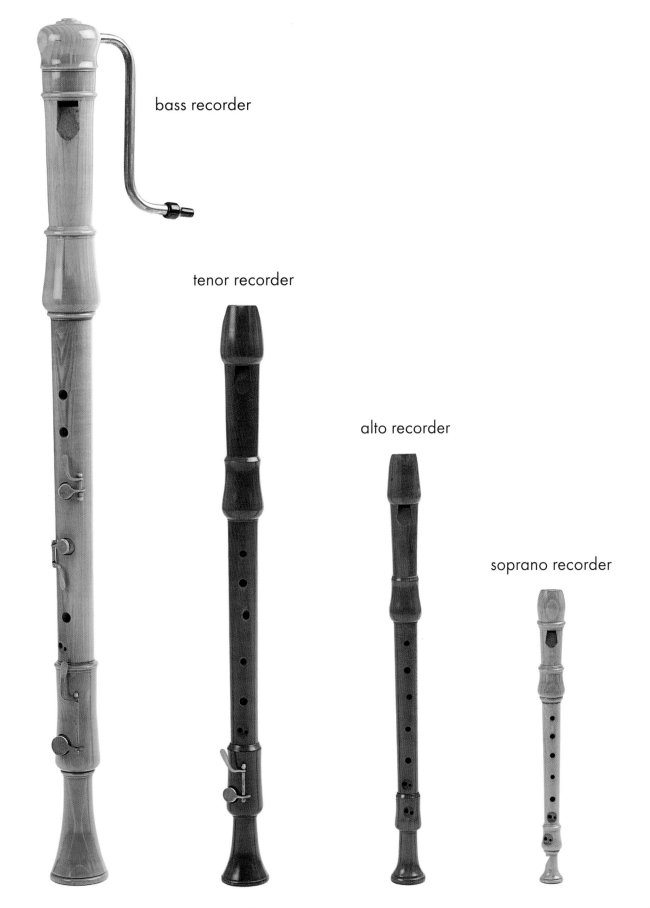

bass recorder

tenor recorder

alto recorder

soprano recorder

CHAPTER EIGHT

The Sound

Recorders can make all kinds of sounds. Sometimes they sound like birds. Sometimes they sound like people singing. They can even sound like spaceships. They are used to play very old music and music that is quite modern.

❮ *It takes some practice, but you can learn to make lots of different sounds on the recorder.*

Instruments such as recorders are played all over the world. They make music that is happy or sad, quiet or lively. What kind of tune would you play?

Other Woodwind Instruments

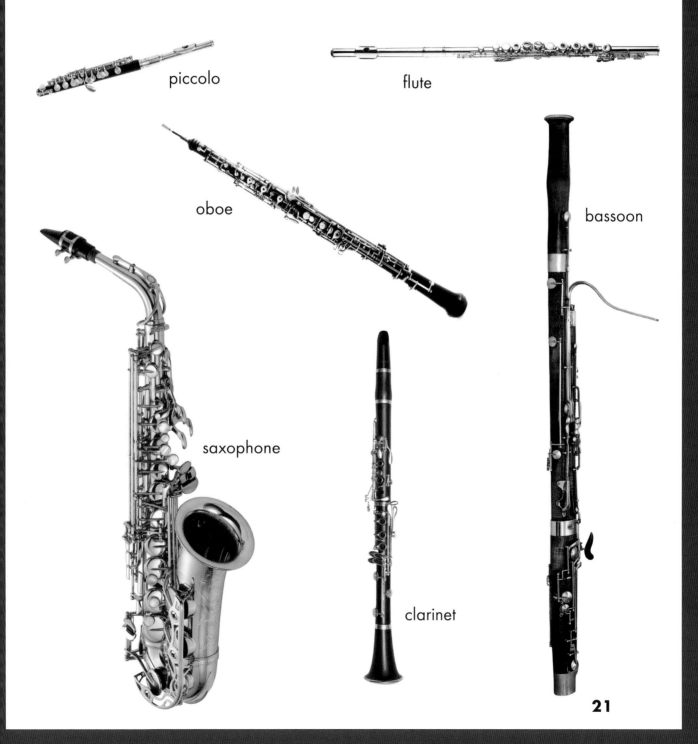

piccolo

flute

oboe

bassoon

saxophone

clarinet

Glossary

bell (BEL): The bottom section of a recorder is the bell. Air flows out of the bell.

block (BLAHK): The block is the part of the mouthpiece that guides air to the place that makes it vibrate.

Middle Ages (MID-ul AY-jez): The Middle Ages was a period of time from about 475 AD to around 1400 AD.

mouthpiece (MOWTH-PEECE): A recorder's mouthpiece is the part the player blows into.

pitch (PICH): In music, pitch is how high or low a sound is.

vibrate (VY-brayt): To vibrate means to move back and forth in a quick way.

woodwinds (WOOD-windz) Woodwinds are tube-shaped instruments that are played by blowing air into a mouthpiece. Recorders are woodwinds.

To Learn More

IN THE LIBRARY

da Silva, Lisete. *How to Play the Recorder.* New York, NY: DK Publishing, 2015.

Nunn, Daniel. *Woodwind.* Chicago, IL: Heinemann Library, 2012.

Pettiford, Rebecca. *Concert.* Minneapolis, MN: Bullfrog Books, 2016.

ON THE WEB

Visit our website for links about recorders:

childsworld.com/links

Note to Parents, Teachers, and Librarians: We routinely verify our Web links to make sure they are safe and active sites. So encourage your readers to check them out!

Index

About the Author

Kara L. Laughlin is an artist and writer who lives in Virginia with her husband, three kids, two guinea pigs, and a dog. She is the author of two dozen nonfiction books for kids.